# From Farm to the Table

Autumn Leigh

Rosen
**REAL**
READERS

Rosen Classroom Books & Materials
New York

1

Corn grows on farms.

Farmers pick the corn.

Trucks take the corn to stores.

Stores sell the corn.

We buy the corn.

We eat the corn!

# Words to Know

corn

farm

farmer

truck